let's pretend!

8 ORIGINAL PIANO SOLOS
BY CAROLYN C. SETLIFF & CATHY DAWSON

ISBN 978-1-4234-2630-1

EXCLUSIVELY DISTRIBUTED BY

WILLIS MUSIC

HAL•LEONARD®

Visit Hal Leonard Online at
www.halleonard.com

Contact us:
Hal Leonard
7777 West Bluemound Road
Milwaukee, WI 53213
Email: info@halleonard.com

In Europe, contact:
Hal Leonard Europe Limited
42 Wigmore Street
Marylebone, London, W1U 2RN
Email: info@halleonardeurope.com

In Australia, contact:
Hal Leonard Australia Pty. Ltd.
4 Lentara Court
Cheltenham, Victoria, 3192 Australia
Email: info@halleonard.com.au

My Bass Drum

Words and Music by Carolyn C. Setliff
and Cathy Dawson

I Am Small

Words and Music by Carolyn C. Setliff
and Cathy Dawson

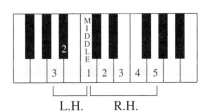

Brightly

(Optional: Play both hands one octave higher)

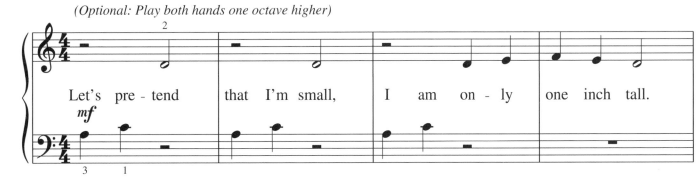

Let's pre - tend that I'm small, I am on - ly one inch tall.

mf

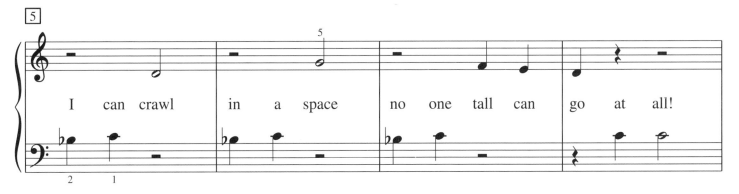

I can crawl in a space no one tall can go at all!

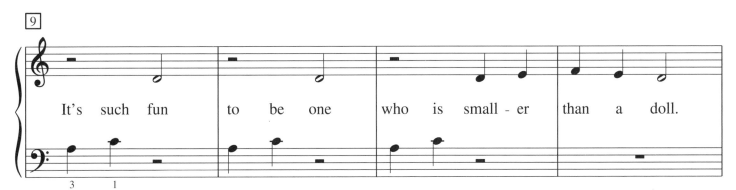

It's such fun to be one who is small - er than a doll.

If I fall, it won't hurt, just 'cause I am ver - y small!

What Would You Think?

Words and Music by Carolyn C. Setliff
and Cathy Dawson

Sailing Along

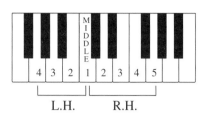

Words and Music by Carolyn C. Setliff
and Cathy Dawson

Relaxed

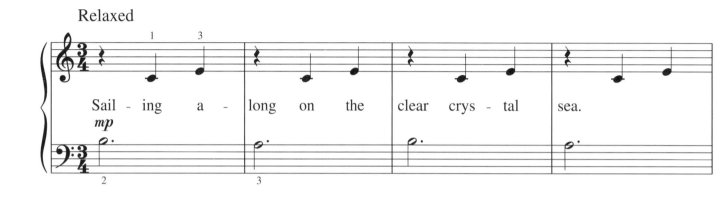

Sail - ing a - long on the clear crys - tal sea.

mp

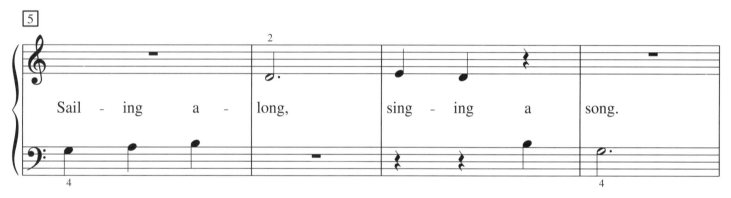

Sail - ing a - long, sing - ing a song.

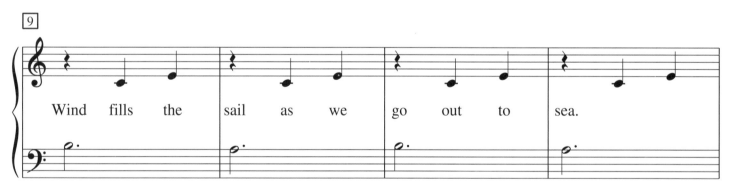

Wind fills the sail as we go out to sea.

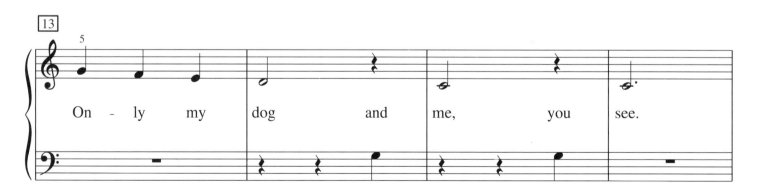

On - ly my dog and me, you see.

It's so much fun to be out in the sun and to

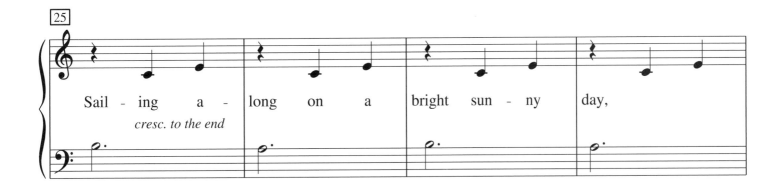

see big white clouds float - ing in the blue sky!

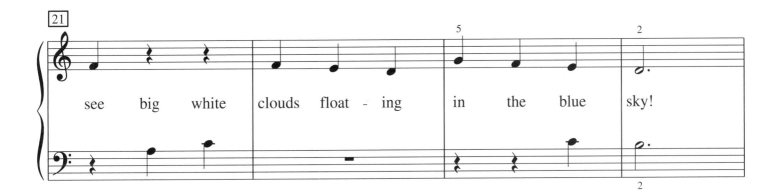

Sail - ing a - long on a bright sun - ny day,
cresc. to the end

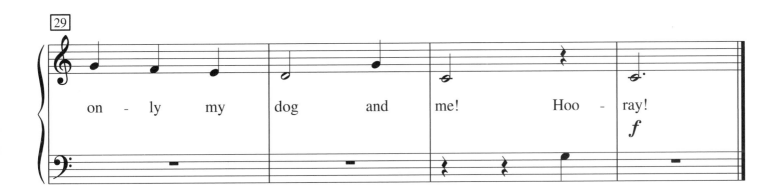

on - ly my dog and me! Hoo - ray!

The Jolly Pirate

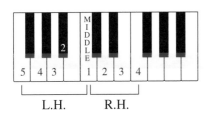

Words and Music by Carolyn C. Setliff
and Cathy Dawson

Boldly

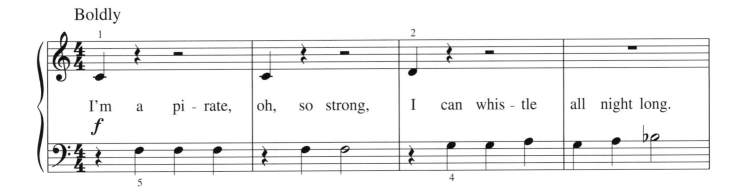

I'm a pi - rate, oh, so strong, I can whis - tle all night long.

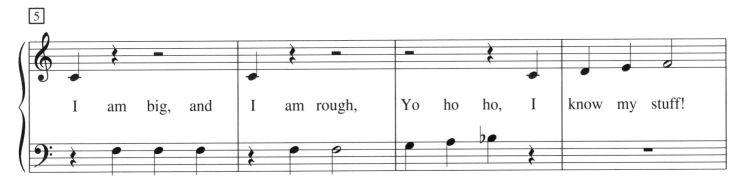

I am big, and I am rough, Yo ho ho, I know my stuff!

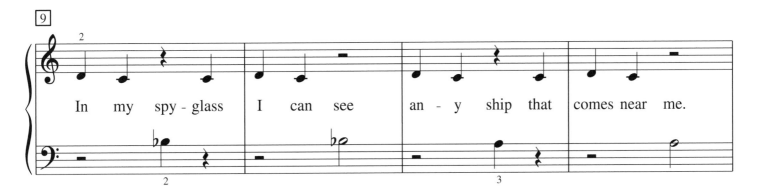

In my spy - glass I can see an - y ship that comes near me.

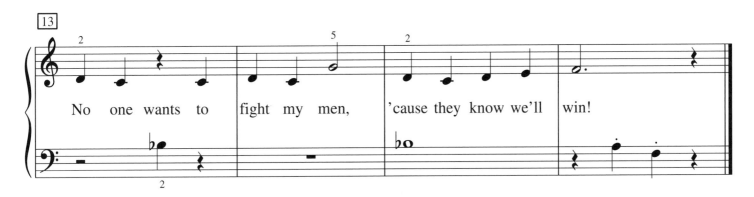

No one wants to fight my men, 'cause they know we'll win!

If Books Could Talk

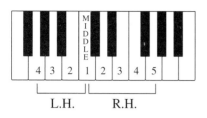

Words and Music by Carolyn C. Setliff
and Cathy Dawson

With imagination

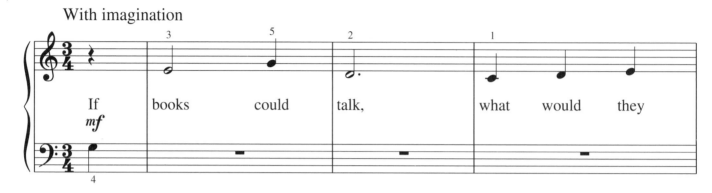

If books could talk, what would they

say? "Come read with me, we'll have a fine

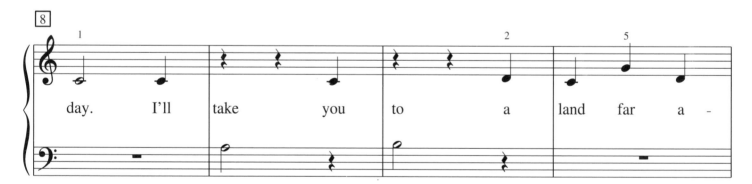

day. I'll take you to a land far a-

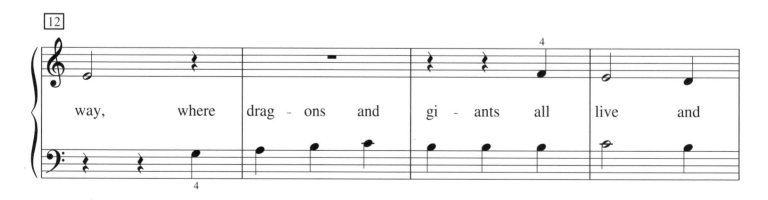

way, where drag - ons and gi - ants all live and

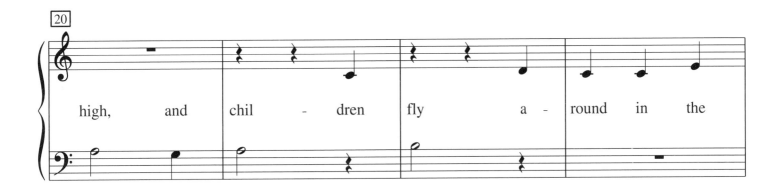

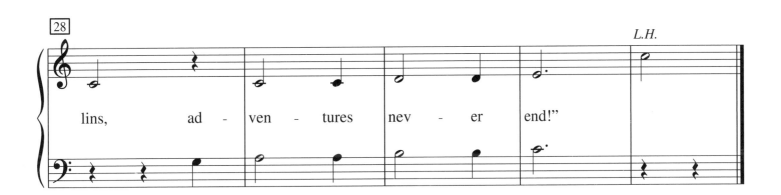

Freight Trains

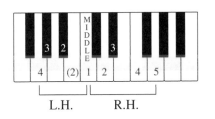

Words and Music by Carolyn C. Setliff
and Cathy Dawson

Chugging along

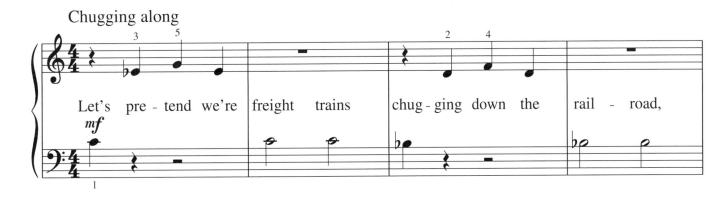

Let's pre - tend we're | freight trains | chug - ging down the | rail - road,

mf

blow - ing our big | whis - tles, | here we | go!

Red ca - boose is | shin - ing, | en - gi - neer is | smil - ing,

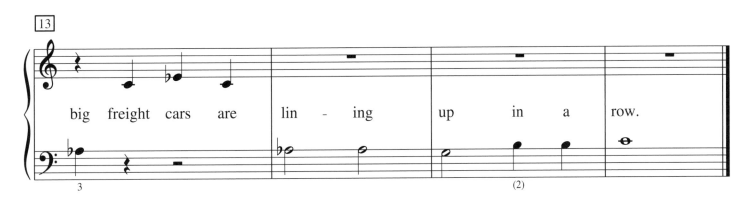

big freight cars are | lin - ing | up in a | row.

The Mad Scientist

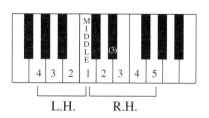

Words and Music by Carolyn C. Setliff
and Cathy Dawson

Not too fast!

I am a mad sci - en - tist, I like to see things bub - ble. But

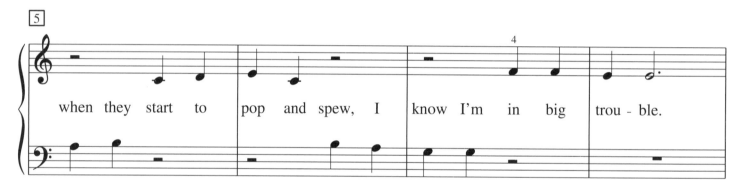

when they start to pop and spew, I know I'm in big trou - ble.

I must be so care - ful what I mix.

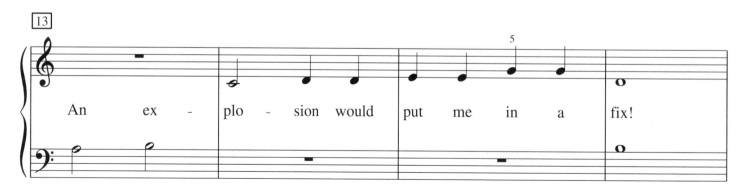

An ex - plo - sion would put me in a fix!

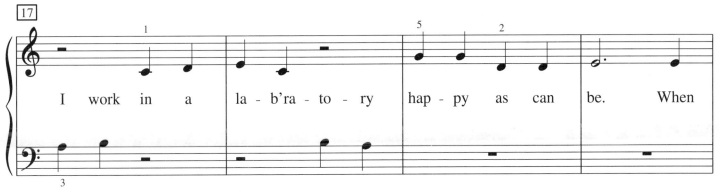

I work in a la- b'ra- to- ry hap- py as can be. When

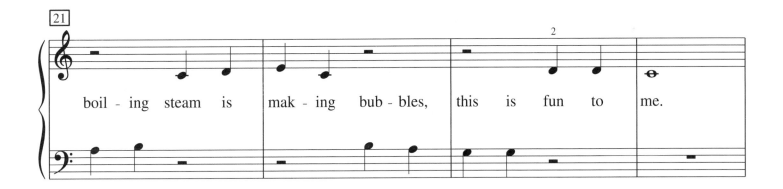

boil - ing steam is mak - ing bub - bles, this is fun to me.

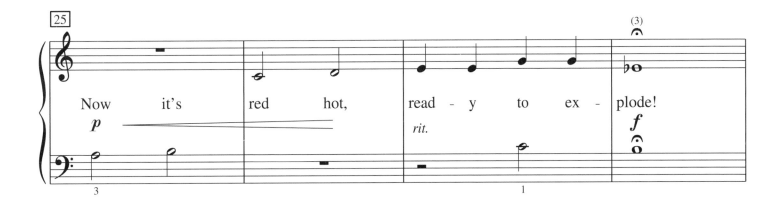

Now it's red hot, ready to ex - plode!

p   *rit.*   *f*

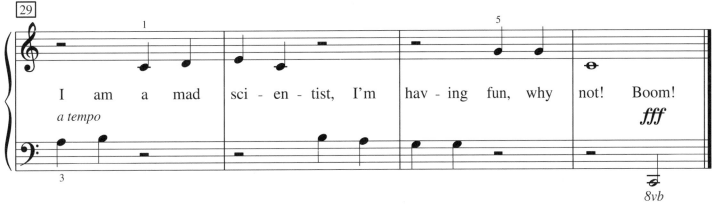

I am a mad sci - en - tist, I'm hav - ing fun, why not! Boom!

a tempo   *fff*

8vb
(Lowest C on piano)

COMPOSER'S CHOICE

The Composer's Choice series showcases piano works by an exclusive group of composers, all of whom are also teachers and performers. Each collection contains 8 original solos and includes classic piano pieces that were carefully chosen by the composer, as well as brand-new compositions written especially for the series. The composers also contributed helpful and valuable performance notes for each collection. Get to know a new Willis composer today!

CLOSER LOOK

View sample pages and hear audio excerpts online at
www.halleonard.com

f @WillisPianoMusic

⊙ willispiano

✗ @WillisPiano

▶ Willis Piano Music

WILLIS MUSIC

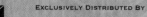

EXCLUSIVELY DISTRIBUTED BY
HAL•LEONARD®
www.willispianomusic.com

Prices, contents, and availability subject to change without notice.

ELEMENTARY

GLENDA AUSTIN
MID TO LATER ELEMENTARY
Betcha-Can Boogie • Jivin' Around • The Plucky Penguin • Rolling Clouds • Shadow Tag • Southpaw Swing • Sunset Over the Sea • Tarantella (Spider at Midnight).
00130168 ....$6.99

CAROLYN MILLER
MID TO LATER ELEMENTARY
The Goldfish Pool • March of the Gnomes • More Fireflies • Morning Dew • Ping Pong • The Piper's Dance • Razz-a-ma-tazz • Rolling River.
00118951 ....$7.99

CAROLYN C. SETLIFF
EARLY TO LATER ELEMENTARY
Dark and Stormy Night • Dreamland • Fantastic Fingers • Peanut Brittle • Six Silly Geese • Snickerdoodle • Roses in Twilight • Seahorse Serenade.
00119289 ....$7.99

INTERMEDIATE

GLENDA AUSTIN
EARLY TO MID-INTERMEDIATE
Blue Mood Waltz • Chromatic Conversation • Etude in E Major • Midnight Caravan • Reverie • South Sea Lullaby • Tangorific • Valse Belle.
00115242 ....$9.99

ERIC BAUMGARTNER
EARLY TO MID-INTERMEDIATE
Aretta's Rhumba • Beale Street Boogie • The Cuckoo • Goblin Dance • Jackrabbit Ramble • Journey's End • New Orleans Nocturne • Scherzando.
00114465 ....$9.99

RANDALL HARTSELL
EARLY TO MID-INTERMEDIATE
Above the Clouds • Autumn Reverie • Raiders in the Night • River Dance • Showers at Daybreak • Sunbursts in the Rain • Sunset in Madrid • Tides of Tahiti.
00122211 ....$8.99

NAOKO IKEDA
EARLY TO MID-INTERMEDIATE
Arigato • The Glacial Mermaid • Land of the Midnight Sun • Sakura • Scarlet Hearts (solo version) • Shooting Stars in Summer • Soft Rain (Azisai) • ...You.
00288891 ....$8.99

CAROLYN MILLER
EARLY INTERMEDIATE
Allison's Song • Little Waltz in E Minor • Reflections • Ripples in the Water • Arpeggio Waltz • Trumpet in the Night • Toccata Semplice • Rhapsody in A Minor.
00123897 ....$8.99